# RELATIONSHIP

## *with a*

# PURPOSE

# RELATIONSHIP

*with a*

# PURPOSE

## How to Have Successful Christ-Centered Relationships

Antonio R. Matthews

*Relationship With a Purpose: How to Have Successful Christ-Centered Relationships*
Published by ZION Publishing House
Sioux Falls, SD & Washington, D C
www.zionpublishinghouse.com

ISBN: 978-1-7323520-8-7

# DEDICATION

To my late grandmother, Carrie Sykes-Boone, for introducing her children to the Lord, and that knowledge and blessing continues to this day.

To my late brothers, Ralph and Mike, for teaching me much about life.

To my late biological father, Ralph Matthews, Sr., for the wonderful times we did share. I was most thankful when you came to stay with me.

To my late mother and father in-love, Fred Hamlin and Bernice Hamlin, for trusting me to love and care for your daughter 'til death do us part.'

To my late "Pop," Mr. Frank Cannon, for showing me how to be a man and to provide for my family. I was paying close attention, sir.

To my first Pastor, the late Verlean Boone of Miracle Temple Church– thank you for setting an amazing example in demonstrating the love and power of God. You will never be forgotten; you've done too much good.

# CONTENTS

# INTRODUCTION

This book is about relationships and how to properly relate to others. In it, I discuss the key relationships in your life and help you to have a complete and correct understanding about these relationships. I am not claiming to be an expert on relationships; however, I now know through experience what was missing in my ability to relate to others in a more profound and honorable way—God, Jehovah.

It's an amazing and awakening experience, that transpires, when you have a true relationship with God the Father. You receive great revelation on the ideal of relationships, and your perspective is totally different than before. As your relationship grows with the Father, so does your understanding and knowledge of Him and how He wants you to relate to others.

To be honest, we won't know how to relate to others without the Father teaching us how to relate to Him first. I do believe this is primarily why so many relationships have failed because people do not have the right knowledge of how to relate to one another. We've all engaged in relationships based on our own limited and inaccurate understanding that we've operated in without the Father's help.

Consider the damage done in family relationships over the years—siblings against siblings; children against parents; cousins against cousins; nieces and nephews against uncles and aunts. Disrespecting my aunts and uncles was never a consideration for me. What in the world has changed that allows this kind of disrespect to be normal?

I've never seen so much turmoil in relationships than I've seen in the past few years; and if we don't correct this lack of understanding of how to relate, it will only get worse. It will continue to the next generation, and so forth, and so on.

Unfortunately, this is a disheartening truth I know firsthand. When the pioneers in my family went home to be with the Lord, division, disrespect, and dysfunction seemed to take over. The turmoil I see now in family relationships is absolutely the opposite of what I used to see. But, I am reminded, if we would seek the Lord with our hearts, He will deliver us from this wickedness and bring such a great change in our ability to relate – it will surely improve our relationships. That is something only God can do.

Even though I have witnessed negative experiences in relationships, I have also experienced the beautiful blessing that happens within godly relationships that reflect heaven on earth. It honors and promotes the purpose of relationship by allowing the Holy Spirit to grace, strengthen, teach, guide, and help you do what is most necessary, and that is to love unconditionally, full of mercy and love—always ready to forgive. "*For thou, Lord, art good, and ready to forgive; and plenteous in mercy unto all them that call upon thee"* Psalm 86:5 (King James Version).

# CHAPTER 1

## ~THE FOUNDATION OF EVERY RELATIONSHIP~

What is the most important relationship? Is it between a husband and a wife, a parent and a child, between siblings, between friends, between an employer and an employee, or is it between co-workers? All of those are important relationships, but *the* most important relationship is between mankind and Jehovah God, the Holy Father.

What if I told you there is a remedy to stop all divorces and to mend every broken relationship? Would you apply that information to your life immediately? I believe you would want to mend all broken relationships, so you could enjoy them to the fullest.

To get a better understanding of what I mean, we'll have to go back to the very beginning to the first relationship between man (Adam) and God, Jehovah.

### The First Relationship

> *Then the Lord God formed man from the dust of the ground and breathed into his nostrils the breath or spirit of life, and man became a living being.* Genesis 2:7, (Amplified Bible, Classic Edition)

When God created man (Adam) in His own image, it was expected that man would have a relationship with God. That's what God intended, and that's how it was before the involvement of sin. Adam and God had a very intimate relationship where they would walk together and talk together while God would explain to Adam all that belonged to him. God loved Adam so much that He gave Adam the privilege to name all the animals in the earth.

> *And out of the ground the Lord God formed every beast of the field, and every fowl of the air; and brought them unto Adam to see what he would call them: and whatsoever Adam called every living creature, that was the name thereof. And Adam gave names to all cattle, and to the fowl of the air, and to every beast of the field; but for Adam there was not found a help meet for him.* Genesis 2:19, 20 (KJV)

This intimate relationship between Adam and God was extremely important to both. It was vital to Adam to maintain this relationship with God, so he would know how to care for the things God entrusted to him. It was important to God because He wanted to express His love toward man. He is an awesome, loving God who wants to express His love at all times.

It is so important to fellowship with God. Fellowship strengthens your relationship and allows God to demonstrate His love toward you. "*And to make all men see what is the fellowship of the mystery, which from the beginning of the world hath been hid in God, who created all things by Jesus Christ:"* Ephesians 3:9 (KJV).

Their relationship was whole, and all was well. It was a *personal relationship* (daily communication, upfront and face to face dialogue) between Adam, Eve, and God. It was only after Adam and Eve sinned that the relationship between man and God ruptured.

In Genesis 3:8, in the Message Bible, it states:

> *When they heard the sound of God strolling in the garden in the evening breeze, the Man and his Wife hid in the trees of the garden, hid from God.*

Notice what happened after they sinned; immediately, they hid themselves when God was coming to commune with them (to have a daily communication, an upfront face to face dialogue.)

## The Impact of a Broken Relationship

A broken relationship with God is what Adam and Eve experienced in the Garden of Eden because of their sin. A broken relationship with God hinders you and robs you of experiencing the Father's excellent grace to properly fulfill every relationship known to man. In Isaiah 26:7, in the Amplified Bible, it states, *"The way of the [consistently] righteous (those living in moral and spiritual rectitude in every area and relationship of their lives) is level and straight; You, O [Lord], Who are upright, direct aright*

*⌐⌐. ke level the path of the [uncompromisingly] just and*
*righteous."*

Parable

*Let's say a father has five children. He loves all of them, but
one child really likes to spend time with his/her father. The
child always likes to go where his/her father goes. Overtime,
this relationship seems to flourish a little more between the
father and this child than the others. Some of the benefits of this
child spending precious time with the father includes things
such as treats, gifts, and other pleasures. Now, outwardly, it
may seem that the father favors this child more than the others.
In reality, an intimate relationship has been cultivated on
purpose because of the child's heart's desire to spend time with
his/her father.*

So, it is with us as children of our heavenly Father. When
we have a desire to spend quality time with the Father,
we will experience great benefits and great favor because
of our relationship with Him.

If your relationship with the Father is not intact
however, then all your other relationships will suffer in
some way or another. You will not know how to properly
relate to others if your relationship with the Father is
broken.

## Being Healed and Restored in Relationships

I want you to use your imagination. What would
it feel like if someone became totally overwhelmed

emotionally because of the most devastating event to ever happen in their life? Normally, when someone is overcome emotionally, it triggers multiple, debilitating effects on their entire being.

I believe what Adam and Eve experienced because of their sin and separation from God, was not only traumatizing, but it left them both very confused and extremely vulnerable. Think about it. All they knew was love, joy, happiness, and peace. All was well and beautiful; and then, out of nowhere, all at once they were unexpectedly introduced to and consumed with despair, depression, shame, humiliation, guilt – the list can go on and on, but I'm sure you understand where I am going with this.

The Bible says in the third chapter of Genesis, verse eight, they both hid themselves from the presence of God. But, the perfect love of the Father pursued them and repositioned them back to their rightful place with Him. Here is where I believe they received their awesome healing – it was through a continual relationship with the Father. First, the healing was them being restored back to the Father. Second, the healing was them being restored back to one another. This healing was absolutely necessary for many reasons – but the main reason was the continuation of God's plan.

## Reflection

*Considering the hurt, shame, and guilt that Adam and Eve experienced that caused them to hide from God, what are some issues from your past that are having a negative impact on your life and in your relationships, that you need to give to God? He is the God of all comfort, and all your healing comes through an intimate relationship with Him.*

Let's pray:

*Father, I make the exchange to give You all my shame, guilt, and condemnation – to receive Your love, righteousness, and joy, as promised in Your word. From this day forward, I will declare that I am restored to Your righteousness and love.*

*Amen*

Now that we have laid down an understanding of how important it is to first have a relationship with God, let us be mindful and thankful of how it will also have a heavenly effect on your other relationships as well. Throughout the Bible, God has given us laws, guidelines, and instructions that have a direct impact on our relationships.

## The Purpose of Relationships

While studying the different godly relationships in the Bible, I found one commonality among them all— they seemed to advance the person in the will of God. For example, consider the supernatural experience a widow gained when the prophet Elijah came to her home

(See 1Kings 17:9-16). She thought her and her son would die after she prepared what she expected to be their very last meal. But after trusting and obeying the words of Elijah, God performed a miracle in her home.

I believe it is God's will that we live in the supernatural not just experience it. That first supernatural experience prepared her for her next supernatural experience. In 1 Kings 17:17-24, that same woman's son dies. And once again, God worked another miracle using Elijah to bring the woman's son back to life. These two wonderful miracles this widow woman experienced had a major impact in her life – it advanced her in the will of God, which is to experience the supernatural as a way of living.

I also noticed **the purpose of a relationship is to protect, promote, and provide**. As I've studied the scriptures, I've noticed multiple relationships where there were either protections, promotions, and/or provisions made within that relationship.

For example, in the relationship between Abram and Lot (uncle and nephew), protection and provision were provided to Lot. In Genesis 14:12-16, (KJV), it reads:

> *And they took Lot, Abram's brother's son, who dwelt in Sodom, and his goods, and departed. And there came one that had escaped and told Abram the Hebrew; for he dwelt in the plain of Mamre the Amorite, brother of*

*Eshcol, and brother of Aner: and these were confederate with Abram. And when Abram heard that his brother was taken captive, he armed his trained servants, born in his own house, three hundred and eighteen, and pursued them unto Dan. And he divided himself against them, he and his servants, by night, and smote them, and pursued them unto Hobah, which is on the left hand of Damascus. And he brought back all the goods, and also brought again his brother Lot, and his goods, and the women also, and the people.*

In the relationship between Moses and Jethro (son in-law and father in-law), protection and promotion were provided to Moses. The wisdom Jethro shared with Moses preserved Moses' life; and as a result, promotion was made to the people. In Exodus 18:14-26, Jethro advised Moses to select a few men to deal with any small disputes, and any significant disputes, Moses would deal with. Moses, taking heed to this advice, allowed some of the men to be promoted and afforded protection for Moses.

In the relationship between Naomi and Ruth (mother in-law and daughter in-law), protection and provision were provided to Ruth. Through Ruth's faithfulness to Naomi, she received provision and protection when she married Boaz. In the relationship between David and Jonathan (friends), there was demonstrated protection, promotion, and provision. Jonathan would often warn David of the danger that was coming his way.

The reason I specified the affiliated titles in these relationships (e.g. in-laws, uncle, nephew, and friends), is to show a common interest between the parties involved. Aside from Abram and Lot, who had some issues, the others had much more respectable relationships which glorified God. This reiterates my point—when we become part of a relationship where Jesus is Lord and in the center of that relationship, the relationship will provide protection, promotion, and provision.

As I mentioned earlier, relationships advance you in the will of God. Let me explain further. Notice how each relationship fulfilled its obligation either to protect, promote, and/or provide. Essentially, it continues those individuals in the will of God for their lives. What if Moses had not received the wisdom he received from Jethro? He probably would have become discouraged, overwhelmed, or even died due to the heavy weight of responsibility he was under. What if Ruth had not been faithful to Naomi? She would have missed out on her blessings, including marrying Boaz. What if David and Jonathan would have ignored the call of God on their lives? David's life would not have been spared as many times, and Jonathan's son, Mephibosheth, would not have benefitted from the covenant that David and Jonathan made to one another.

Therefore, it is so important to know the purpose of relationships and then cultivate relationships with other believers in Christ. As believers in Christ, we ought to be able to advance each other in the will of God.

Testimony:

*In 2010, I decided to attend Victory Bible College (VBC) in Suitland, MD. VBC is a school inside the church I attend called Victory Christian Ministries International. My reason for attending this school was to further my knowledge and relationship with the Father. After making the decision to attend VBC, I began experiencing an attack on my family that challenged my decision to attend Bible college. I met with a deacon at my church, he shared an encouraging word with me, and we prayed. Not only did I continue the mission to attend Victory Bible College, I graduated with a bachelor's degree in religious studies. Can you see how this deacon, allowing God to use him, advanced me in the will of God?*

Testimony:

*In 2015, I was tested in tithing. There was a major increase for my health insurance coverage with my employer that affected my salary as well as my tithing. Not paying tithes bothered me for months. Finally, I spoke with an elder of the church. He encouraged me with scriptures and a personal testimony. He then prayed with me. What he shared with me advanced me in the will of God, and since that day, I have been paying my tithes regularly. I'm glad I went to the elder to receive encouraging words about tithing. If I had gone to someone else, that person might not have had the maturity as a Christian to advance me in God's will. In other words, he/she might have said something to the effect, "You don't have to pay your tithes this time, and God knows your heart." Although this person means well, the truth of the matter is his/her words could very well be a hindrance to me, as it pertains to my walk in faith.*

When we think of relationships, the core principle for us to consider should be how we are relating to each other. This is where we need to transition from the inaccurate information that we've come to believe, toward a more meaningful, purposeful understanding of how to properly relate to one another God's way.

If anyone is in any kind of relationship, without having an intimate relationship with God, that relationship, without a doubt, will fail. With all the many broken relationships in our society today, it will take God's love to mend and heal us completely, This He can do, but only through intimate fellowship, which once again strengthens relationships.

## Kingdom-Minded Relationships

All relationships are not good for you nor are they all needed. This alone is why it is so important to establish a *heart to heart* relationship with God, the Father. Let Him lead you to the right relationships. Relationships should be all about ministering to others or being ministered to.

In Proverbs 27:17 in the Amplified Bible, Classic Edition, it states, *"Iron sharpens iron; so a man sharpens the*

*countenance of his friend [to show rage or worthy purpose].*"
Can you see the ministering implication in this scripture?
If I am your friend, I should be able to make you better
not tear you down or help with some form of self-
destruction.

Think of it like this: the difference between a
kingdom-minded person and a person who is not
kingdom-minded is life or death.

Case in point: Let's say a couple is having
difficulties in their relationship. The person who is not
kingdom-minded might consider drinking, drugs, and/or
sex with another person as a way to deal with their
marital problems. All these things equal death or
separation from God.

The kingdom-minded person would approach it a
totally different way because of who they are, and who
they have become. The Word of God has enabled them to
sow life into every situation. The kingdom-minded
person will minister to you. Ask God to give you friends
who are kingdom-minded and separate yourself from
those who are not kingdom-minded. Pray for those who
are not kingdom-minded, and where appropriate,
minister to them by letting God's glory shine through
you.

Having a kingdom mind-set comes with
tremendous benefits. In Psalm 68:19 (KJV), it says,
*"Blessed be the Lord, who daily loadeth us with benefits, even
the God of our salvation. Selah."*

One of these benefits is PEACE. This peace acts like a shield that protects your mind from all disturbances. In Philippians 4:7 KJV), it says, *"And the peace of God, which passeth all understanding, shall keep your hearts and minds through Christ Jesus."*

This peace is like no other peace on earth. Jesus said in John 14:27 (KJV), - *"Peace I leave with you, my peace I give unto you: not as the world giveth, give I unto you. Let not your heart be troubled, neither let it be afraid."* Notice how Jesus said He gives His Peace unto you, not the (peace) the world gives. The world's peace is full of destruction.

### *Reflection*

*Do you have anyone who can provide you with biblical advice that would advance you in the will of God for your life? If not, ask the Father to send believers with a kingdom mind-set who can advance you in the will of God.*

# CHAPTER 2

## ~EMBRACING A SUPERNATURAL LIFESTYLE~

**The Elijah Effect**

After establishing an intimate relationship with the Father where trust and confidence in His true love for you has become your heavenly reality, you now have an assurance that no matter how difficult a situation may start, or the process you may go through – this intimate relationship with the Father comforts you that all things will work for your good. He is *"the God of all comfort."* 2 Corinthians 1:3 (KJV)

It is at this point you learn how to journey with the Father. This is where it is extremely important that you experience victories while walking in faith. Every victory you experience in faith gives you supernatural momentum and strengthens your walk in Christ. Living from faith to faith while experiencing victories along the way brings the Father much joy and delight. This is the supernatural lifestyle we are to live. It is the Father who sustains you supernaturally. In 1 Kings 17:1-24, Elijah experienced multiple supernatural situations where the Father provided what was needed to sustain him. Each situation was extremely challenging, yet it revealed how much Elijah trusted the Father to provide for him.

Your trust in the Father when challenged with a difficult situation will increase your faith, which in turn will result in advancement for your life. Every small victory of walking in supernatural faith sustains you and prepares you for your next challenge in life. I like to call it, "The Elijah Effect."

## Man's Perspective versus Supernatural Man's Perspective

A right relationship with the Father supersedes a natural way of living. There is a difference between a *man's perspective* and a *supernatural man's perspective*. This impacts how you relate with both the Father and with people.

A *man's perspective* is one that only views things according to the five senses, which are seeing, hearing, smelling, touching, and tasting. Human reasoning can also be affected negatively when attempting to live a supernatural lifestyle. For example, human reasoning factors the outcome to your ability; what *you* can do, which is limited. However, faith depends on God, completely, for the outcome—what *He* can do. What He is able to do is limitless.

For further understanding, consider the story of Mary, the mother of Jesus. The gospel of Luke 1:28-38, talks about an encounter between an angel and Mary. The angel said to Mary that she would bring forth a son, and she should name him, Jesus. Listen to Mary's initial reaction in verse 34, (KJV) *"Then said Mary unto the angel, How shall this be, seeing I know not a man?"* This was her natural, human reaction. The first thing Mary considered was the fact that she had never had sexual relations with a man, so naturally, she'd question her natural ability to be pregnant. However, when God says He is going to do something for you, in you, or through you, it is not based on your ability. He will provide all things necessary for whatever He said He would do. Therefore, faith is extremely necessary to receive from God. Human reasoning can hinder you from receiving because the natural mind cannot truly or fully understand the things of God.

Verse 38 reveals Mary's faith at work. When she came to the realization that she should simply **accept** what God wanted to do she said,

> ...*As his servant, I* **accept** *whatever he has for me. May everything you have told me come to pass." And the angel left her.*

The Passion Translation

The King James version puts it like this,

> *And Mary said, Behold the handmaid of the Lord; be it unto me according to thy word. And the angel departed from her.*

When a believer attempts to live by faith, *man's perspective* will always present struggles. Hebrews 11:1 teaches us that, *faith is the substance of things hoped for, the evidence of things not seen.* (KJV)

How can one live by faith and *man's perspective* at the same time? As a believer, whenever you try to apply *man's perspective* where only faith should apply, it creates struggles and much frustration.

Let me provide you with a biblical example from II Kings 6:15-17 in the Easy-to-Read Version:

*Elisha's servant got up early that morning. When he went outside, he saw an army with horses and chariots all around the city. The servant said to Elisha, "Oh, my master, what can we do?" Elisha said, "Don't be afraid. The army that fights for us is larger than the army that fights for Aram." Then Elisha prayed and said, "LORD, I ask you, open my servant's eyes so that he can see." The LORD opened the eyes of the young man, and the servant saw the mountain was full of horses and chariots of fire. They were all around Elisha.*

In verse 15, Elisha's servant saw through his natural *man's perspective* what appeared to be trouble. But, then Elisha encouraged him not to be afraid, and then said to him, "the army that fights for us is larger than the army that fights for Aram." This is an example of a *supernatural man's perspective* which always gives you heaven's perspective in a situation. In verse 17, Elisha prayed for the servant that the Lord would give him sight to see—*supernatural man's perspective*—and the Lord opened the young man's eyes, and he was able to see.

Elisha was instrumental in advancing this man into God's will for his life. It was good that the servant knew someone with a *supernatural man's perspective* to go to which furthered him into the will of God. Everyone cannot advance you into the will of God for your life because everyone does not have a *supernatural man's perspective.*

It is God's desire and His will that believers, not only experience the supernatural but also live in it. Supernatural perspective allows you to walk in God's ultimate plans for your life just as the Bible expresses it.

## Living Supernaturally, Naturally

In general, living naturally requires lots of practice over time to get the desired result. The more you practice, the better you get. The less you practice, the worse you perform. Let's use sports as an example. If you miss too many practices, chances are you might not play in the game nor do well in the competition. It always shows up during the competition who has had sufficient practice and who has not. I learned this difficult lesson in my younger years as a boxer. If you didn't get your road work in (running), you would have tired early in sparring. Sometimes to teach you a lesson, the coach would allow the sparring to continue past your tolerance level as a form of punishment for showing up unprepared.

The same principles and concepts apply when learning to live supernaturally. Although it is by God's grace that we grow in faith (Ephesians 2:8), we must practice what is most precious and necessary to sustain our walk in Christ, and that awesome experience is only gained through an intimate relationship with the Father.

In over thirty years' experience as a believer, what I've learned to be most precious and necessary to me in this Christian walk is consistently speaking God's word over my life and everything that pertains to my life. Study His word with the help of the Holy Spirit, expecting to receive revelation and impartation. Begin to acknowledge God quickly and immediately, especially when your faith is challenged. *"In all thy ways acknowledge him, and He shall direct thy paths."* Proverbs 3:6 (KJV). In my experiences with this truth, I've realized that when I acknowledge GOD in my challenges, I am immediately comforted, reassured, and His peace envelops me.

Testimony:

*In October 2012, I was wrongfully removed from my employment. When fear and anxiety tried to grip me, I quickly set my thoughts and my affection on the Lord. I also continued my daily fellowship with the Lord and my weekly fellowship with Christian brethren at the church. As my strength was renewed, I realized this truth—when you're confronted with challenges, the enemy's plan is to first separate you from the Father and then from the brethren. He wants to stop your fellowship, so that he can isolate you to himself, ultimately destroying you and everything you believe.*

*There were so many wonderful blessings that occurred during this time of learning and developing my faith in the Lord.*
***First,*** *by setting my entire being in alignment with the Lord and not being troubled by what was going on, I was able to hear from the Holy Spirit and be led to make the right decisions. I acknowledged the Lord that he might guide my footsteps (Proverbs 3:6).*

***Second,*** *I maintained my fellowship with the brethren. This is where my next blessing showed up. One day while ushering, a gentleman and his wife walked down my aisle to be seated. As I ushered him and his wife to their seats, he said to me, "Every time my wife and I come down your aisle, you're always so nice to us. Here's my card; if you need anything, call me." On his business card, described the kind of work I do. I believe this was the first time the thought came to me, "God, You're so funny!" I believe that I was at the right place at that right time. What if I had allowed the negative experience of being wrongfully terminated keep me away from fellowship? I would have missed out on my blessing.*

***Third,*** *the gentleman who gave me his card was very instrumental in me getting my next job with the National Geographic Museum in Washington D.C. My very first day on the job as I was getting off, I was met by a total stranger. Within minutes into our conversation, he shared with me that he was having trouble in his marriage. Immediately, I thought* *to myself, who set this up? I felt like I was looking around, asking myself, who set this up? After coming back to myself, I began ministering to him about his marriage. When I finally got to my vehicle, I realized my purpose at this new job. I submitted myself to the Father and said whatever You need me to do, wherever You need me to go, and whomever You need me to minister to – You have my permission to move me about. The six months I was there at this place, ministry was always at the forefront. There were healings, restorations, and deliverances which happened within that time frame. You could honestly sense there was a refreshing of God's presence in that place. The testimonies shared were quite reassuring and most humbling.*

In August 2013, *Abba* Father opened a door, and I returned to my previous job with all my time and leave restored, and I also was given an increase in my pay. I guess you could say my work there at the National Geographic Museum was done, and it was time for me to return.

### Study to show yourself approved

*Find a biblical character that operated in the supernatural when his or her faith was tested.*

# CHAPTER 3

## ~LEARNING HOW TO RELATE WITH OTHERS~

Relating to Your Spouse: Learning to "Spouse One Another"

> *Therefore shall a man leave his father and his mother and shall cleave unto his wife: and they shall be one flesh.* Genesis 2:24 (KJV)

> *Husbands, love your wives, even as Christ also loved the church, and gave himself for it.* Ephesians 5:25 (KJV)

Ephesians, Chapter 5, verse 25 is an awesome scripture. The question is, how can a husband love his wife as Christ loved the church? He cannot do this without Christ in his life. Getting revelation knowledge on this simple truth will full-proof your marriage against divorce.

When a man marries a woman, they become one flesh. He now must love her as he loves himself. He must give himself up or lay his life down for her sake. In other words, he should love her so unconditionally that he is no longer motivated by how he feels, but everything he does for her is simply because he has chosen to do so.

Isn't it interesting how feelings can dictate how a husband or wife may treat their spouse—determining when they are worthy of a good deed?

Contrary to popular belief, love is not based on feelings. If that is what love is, then every time a husband or wife gets upset with each other, a lot of wonderful expressions, kind words, or acts of love will not be demonstrated. Most couples, when they are upset with each other, don't want to be bothered with one another. This causes them to suffer unnecessary, debilitating anger which causes them to be disturbed, affecting their relationship.

Years ago, when my wife and I first got married, whenever there was a disturbance, or a verbal altercation, I would immediately grab my wife and hold her in my arms affectionately, and say to her, "I'm not going to let you go until you hug me back." Well, what I learned or gained from that experience is that my action literally stopped what possibly could have been numerous onslaughts of the *enemy's attacks* against my marriage. Think about it, every time a husband and wife spend time arguing and being mad at each other, it robs them of precious moments they could be sharing with one another.

God's principles for marriage are still best, and nothing else can compare; nothing even comes close. I got married in 1989. In 2010, I realized that my wife was absolutely graced to "spouse me." Now we're "spousing" each other, or as I like to call it, we're "spousing" out.

~Spousing is my creative word I like to use to describe how my wife and I interact with each other. I, particularly, love the way she meets me with the help I need and how she encourages me when I am dealing with difficult situations. She is my perfect gift to me, and therefore, I do my best to spoil her and show my love to her continuously. We're spousing each other.

When Adam first met his wife, he said sweet, beautiful words about her, *based on how he viewed her.* In Genesis 2:23, Adam said, *"This is now bone of my bones, and flesh of my flesh; She shall be called Woman, because she was taken out of Man"* (New King James Version).

When the enemy got involved, he changed Adam's view of Eve. In Genesis 3:12, Adam said, *"And the man said, the woman whom thou gavest to be with me, she gave me of the tree, and I did eat"* (KJV). Not the same endearing words he first said of Eve. Whenever married couples allow the enemy to involve himself -the view of one another changes quickly; subsequently, the marriage becomes troubled and jeopardized.

God has called the wife to the be the husband's "helpmeet." A helpmeet is a wife who meets her husband with the help he needs. Her help can be reassuring, comforting, loving, nurturing, and directional. Yes, she can even help a husband to make the right decisions. However, if a husband neglects his wife, he cuts himself off from whatever good she can be to him. When a wife is not honored, loved, respected, or valued - she cannot fulfill her rightful role as a helpmeet.

If a husband does not yield to his helpmeet – he cannot hear from the Holy Spirit. In 1 Peter 3:7 Amplified Bible (AMP) it reads,

> *In the same way, you husbands, live with your wives in an understanding way [with great gentleness and tact, and with an intelligent regard for the marriage relationship], as with someone physically weaker, since she is a woman. Show her honor and respect as a fellow heir of the grace of life, so that your prayers will not be hindered or ineffective."*

When a husband neglects to heed or yield to his helpmeet (his wife), he is robbing himself of the goodness that she has been created to provide to him. When a wife (helpmeet) is not allowed to honor her role, she cannot fulfill her purpose as a wife

God has called the husband to love his wife like Christ loved the church. A husband's sacrifice is to give himself up for his wife. To my wife, it's my duty to make her feel honored, respected, and loved in our marriage. I yield to what she has to share when decisions are made in our home. I make sure she knows her value to my family. I honor her role as my helpmeet; therefore, I receive all the good she was purposed to be. In Proverbs 18:22, in The Voice (VOICE) it reads,

*The man who finds a wife finds something good, and the favor of the Eternal is indeed his."* I am the recipient of her goodness. Amen.

Let us pray:

*Father, I thank You for Your word and instructions for a blessed marriage. I pray that every marriage will receive revelation from You on how to enhance their marriage through Your word. I pray that husbands will seek Your face for clarity on how to honor, respect, and love their helpmeet - Amen.*

## Relating to Your Children

*Fathers, don't exasperate your children by coming down hard on them. Take them by the hand and lead them in the way of the Master* Ephesians 6:4 (The Message).

*Fathers, do not irritate and provoke your children to anger [do not exasperate them to resentment], but rear them [tenderly] in the training and discipline and the counsel and admonition of the Lord* (Ephesians 6:4 AMPC).

Isn't it wonderful how God gives you insight, through His word, how to minister to your children? Even in the worst-case scenario, we still are to totally trust our children to Him. As parents, we are to love them unconditionally, and this requires help from the Father.

Whenever you become so frustrated with your child, and you are trying to do all you can to help them, but nothing seems to work; the most important thing you can do is give them over to God, prayerfully, and continue to show them love regardless. The worst thing you can do is constantly irritate them because that will push them away from you.

God's ultimate plan for relationship affects us all toward Him. When you encounter His love, it's without prerequisites – nothing is required to receive His love; He just loves you, and that's the same kind of love He wants us to show toward one another – without prerequisites. This will certainly help you in all your relationships, especially your relationships with your children.

A wonderful and kind act that you can do is to pray with your children. It teaches them to humble themselves unto God and to reverence Him. Take the time to share scriptures with them, and please take them to church where they can hear God's Word, and possibly develop a relationship with other children in church. This can have a positive affect on them.

Let us pray:

*Father, we thank you for our children; they are gifts from You. Your word teaches us how to raise them, correct them, and love them. We are to share Your word with them when we sit down, lie down, rise up, and as we go about our day. Amen.*

### Relating to Your Parents

*Children, obey your parents in all things: for this is well pleasing unto the Lord.* Colossians 3:20 Blue Red and Gold Bible

*Honor thy father and thy mother: that thy days may be long upon the land which the Lord thy God giveth thee.* Exodus 20:12 (BRG) Bible.

It seems, the older children get, the less they obey their parents. I am forty-five years old, and if my mom or pop instructs me to do something, I will obey them; for this is the will of God. My relationship with God compels me to relate to other people, like my parents, as unto Him.

Once your parents have raised you, provided for you, and have done all they can for you, it's so unfortunate that often times when parents age, their children are quick to put their parents away. Now, I understand certain situations might arise where medically or physically you cannot provide the care they desperately need; that's clearly understood. However, if they can come live with you, or if you can assist with ensuring their bills get paid monthly by managing their finances, this would be a great help to them. Checking on them from day to day and making sure they are okay is what God expects you to do; it's honoring His word.

> *Whoso robbeth his father or his mother, and saith, It is no transgression; the same is the companion of a destroyer* Proverbs 28:24 (KJV).

In this scripture, when you think of the word "robbeth", or "rob", don't limit your understanding to physically taking money from your parents, but please consider if you're not rightfully providing the care your parents need – you're robbing them of God's expected love.

> *For Moses said, Honor (revere with tenderness of feeling and deference) your father and your mother, and, He who curses or reviles or speaks evil of or abuses or treats improperly his father or mother, let him surely die. But [as for you] you say, A man is exempt if he tells [his] father or [his] mother, What you would*

*otherwise have gained from me [everything I have that would have been of use to you] is Corban, that is, is a gift [already given as an offering to God], Then you no longer are permitting him to do anything for [his] father or mother [but are letting him off from helping them].* Mark 7:10-12 (AMPC).

God, Jehovah, is not the kind of God that expects you to neglect your parents for any reason. He instructs you to love them and honor them.

Let us pray:

*Father, I thank you for giving us the ability to care for our parents. We are graced to love them and provide to them the same care and compassion you have given unto us, Amen.*

**Relating to Your Brethren**

Having a relationship with the brethren—your brothers and sisters in Christ—is vitally important. It is so important, it can be a matter of life and death. The word of God provides us with several examples of the importance of building community among the Body of Christ.

One thing is for sure- your brethren, whether male or female, will always encourage you in the Lord, as the Word of God instructs us in 1 Thessalonians 5:11,

*Wherefore comfort yourselves together, and edify one another, even as also ye do"* (KJV). Also, in Galatians

6:1 it reads, *"Brethren, if a man be overtaken in a fault, ye which are spiritual, restore such an one in the spirit of meekness; considering thyself, lest thou also be tempted* (KJV).

It is just as important that you establish and continue your fellowship with the brethren, as stated in Hebrews 10:25,

> *Not forsaking the assembling of ourselves together, as the manner of some is; but exhorting one another: and so much the more, as ye see the day approaching* (KJV).

A brother or sister in Christ will not only speak into your life, but they will constantly keep you lifted up in prayer:

> *We are bound to thank God always for you, brethren, as it is meet, because that your faith groweth exceedingly, and the charity of every one of you all toward each other aboundeth* II Thessalonians 1:3 (KJV).

As brethren, we have a genuine concern for one another; for we are our brother's keeper. In Genesis 4:9, Cain asked God a question:

> *"And the LORD said unto Cain, Where is Abel thy brother? And he said, I know not: Am I my brother's keeper?"* (KJV)And the answer is – **Yes, you are.**

In Proverbs 27:17 it reads,

> *Iron sharpeneth iron; so a man sharpeneth the countenance of his friend"* (KJV).

A person becomes a better person when he is in the company of brethren. This is why it is so important that you hang around those who are like you. As a child of God; not only does it strengthen you, it reminds you of who you are, and to whom you belong.

When it comes to being properly advised or instructed in the things of God, a person outside of the will of God cannot serve in this function for you. In Proverbs 11:14 it says, *"Where no counsel is, the people fall: but in the multitude of counsellors there is safety"* (KJV). Without godly counsel, the counsel you do receive can place you outside of the will of God and can actually do more harm than good. On the other hand, a brother or sister who is an anointed man or woman of God, who stands on the Word of God and recognizes it as the final authority in their life, can speak a word into your life, and all of heaven will move on your behalf. This further demonstrates how valuable your brothers and sisters in Christ are.

Let us pray:

*Father, I thank you for the divine relationships that I have. I am very blessed to have Christians to pray for me and to be genuinely concerned about my well-being. You have placed these precious people in my life for Your purpose, to minister to me and to keep me in constant remembrance of who I am in You, Amen.*

## Relating to Associates

There's a saying that goes: *You can tell a lot about a person by whom they hang around.* Would you agree? I certainly agree with this saying. We often have friends we have something in common with or something that appeals to us about certain people.

For example, when I was a young man, I had friends who smoked, drank alcoholic beverages, and loved to party or go to clubs. Those were the same things I used to like to do. But, I also had friends who didn't smoke or drink, but we still had something in common; they liked to party, and they liked women.

Another popular saying: *Birds of the feather flock together.* How many times have you seen a mixed group of birds flocking together? Usually, when they are traveling together, they all look alike. I've never seen anything different. I'm not saying it hasn't happened; I just haven't seen it.

What I am trying to convey is just as birds that flock together usually look like each other, this same principle applies to us. You will most likely hang around friends who have something in common with you or something about them that appeals to you. Here's another popular saying: *Good girls like bad boys.* I'm sure you've heard this one before. This same statement also applies in the reverse—*good guys like bad girls.* There is a foolish curiosity of being in a relationship with a person who lives on the edge or lives carefree. Additionally, people who find themselves in these ill-advised relationships often encounter unnecessary hurt or abuse, whether it be physically and/or emotionally. Think about that.

## Winning Your Associates Over for Christ

Before I fully address this topic, let's first put a fairly common but misconstrued sentiment on the table: *"Jesus didn't have a problem hangin' with sinners." Okay,* now that we've gotten that statement out of the way, let us continue.

It's true. Jesus did hang around sinners; however, it was to glorify God, which brings me to this question: The people you hang around and are in relationship with, do those relationships glorify God? Remember, the name of this book is *"Relationship With a Purpose"* Are your relationships serving His purpose? That is something to think about.

Let me provide some biblical context from John, Chapter 3, where Jesus is explaining to Nicodemus, a religious Jewish leader, that access to the Kingdom of God is not possible unless a person is born again. When Nicodemus came to see Jesus, he asked Him,

> *How can a man be born when he is old? Can he enter the second time into his mother's womb, and be born?"* John 3:4 (KJV).

This entire encounter between Jesus and Nicodemus was strategic, as God was putting Nicodemus on Jesus' playing field—opening the door for Jesus to witness to him about salvation. Read the complete passage in John 3.

I use the term "playing field" because it relates to strategy. Strategy will help you be more effective in battle when it comes to winning the souls of your associates for Christ. For example, let's say you're at work, and you encounter your co-workers in the middle of a not-so-appropriate conversation. Your co-workers continue to discuss whatever they were discussing before you arrived, even with the prior knowledge that you are a Christian and are likely not pleased with the things they are saying. In this instance, you are on their "playing field". However, several weeks later, one of these same co-workers approaches you for prayer. This co-worker will likely come to you in a more respectable manner, being very mindful of what he says around you because he has now entered your "playing field".

Now that we have a better understanding of the term "playing field", it is just as important to know why we, as Christians, ought not to place ourselves in a compromising situation by hanging around certain people or individuals. The most meaningful question you must ask yourself is, *Why do I want to hang around friends or co-workers who drink, smoke, or do drugs?* Does this kind of playing field glorify God? Can you effectively witness to that person or those people without offending them, if you're doing the same things they're doing? The best thing you can do is separate yourself from that kind of environment and allow them to come to you, on your playing field. Meanwhile, let us who are Christians, be very mindful of how we live and conduct ourselves in the presence of others, whether it be in our work place, in our homes, or in our neighborhood. By doing this, we allow God's glory to be revealed unto those that are lost, and like Nicodemus, they too will come to us with questions about salvation, and we can win them over for Christ.

Let us pray:

*Father, we thank You for Your truth. For it reveals to us who we are in You or out of You. I pray that eyes and ears will open to Your truth and that hearts will receive understanding on how to seek and establish only those relationships that will glorify You, Amen.*

## Relating to Our Heavenly Father

Once again, the most important relationship we can ever establish on this earth is the one with our Creator- God, Jehovah. The one true understanding I realized is the more I fellowship with God in His presence, the more He reveals to me who He is. It is in that moment of intimate fellowship that He reveals to me who I am in Him and what my true purpose is on earth. He has even revealed to me things about my family that have come to pass. For example, in February 2010, I told my son he would give his life to the Lord by the end of the year. My son asked me how I knew that. I just said, "You will." Later, that same year in the month of August, I said the same thing to him, "You're going to give your life unto the Lord by the end of this year." He asked the same thing, "Dad, how do you know this?" Well, on November 9, 2010, my wife and I went over to my son's home to discuss with him some things that were troubling him. My son and I went out to my vehicle for a private discussion. During that discussion, after explaining a particular matter, he made a comment that referenced God: He said, "God knows my heart". The Holy Spirit said to me, "Talk to him about that."

So, I said to him that was an interesting statement you just made that God knows your heart. I asked him if he were to die that night, where he would spend eternity. Once again, he said God knew his heart, and he was a good person. He said that he believed he would go to heaven. That's when we discussed the true fact that God does know what's in man's heart, and that being good alone does not get you into heaven. I told him you have to be born again and accept God's salvation for man. We opened the Bible to Romans 10:9-10 where it states,

> *That if thou shalt confess with thy mouth the Lord Jesus, and shalt believe in thine heart that God hath raised him from the dead, thou shalt be saved. For with the heart man believeth unto righteousness; and with the mouth confession is made unto salvation* (KVJ).

Afterwards, my son accepted the Lord Jesus Christ as his personal savior. I humorously reminded him of the two prophetic declarations I made to him that he would give his life to the Lord by the end of the year. As I said before, the date we went over to his home was Nov. 9, 2010. November 10th is my birthday; after my son and I thought about it, we laughed, and laughed, and laughed some more. That's when I said to God, "You're so funny." And, that statement…that comment, "You're so funny" had been mentioned so many times throughout the year 2010. It is so awesome how God can take a statement or a word and make it a part of your life unto Him.

There are so many wonderful benefits fellowshipping with the presence of God. There is fullness of joy, a peace that passes all understanding, and the opportunity for Him to express His wonderful love to you. All of which can only come through fellowship with Him. Can you imagine God communing with you day-by-day, discussing things about your life, even about your family? My prayer is that you will have multiple encounters with the presence of God- to the point where you are literally crying out to God to reveal more of His glory to you. Glory to God! In His Word, it states that if you will seek Him diligently with all your heart, all your mind, and with all your soul, you will find Him. There is so much truth He will reward you with for seeking Him diligently.

Let us pray:

*Father, we thank You for Your word that tells us how much You want to fellowship with us. How we ought to come before Your presence with singing and enter Your courts with praise. Your word tells us we ought to always be thankful, despite of situations or circumstances, knowing that all things work for the good of them that love You, Amen.*

### *Practice acknowledging the Father*

*For seven days acknowledge the Father five times throughout the day; in the morning, in the afternoon, in the mid-evening, in the late evening, and before you go to bed. Simply remind yourself of His goodness and how much He loves you. At the end of the week, reflect on what you experienced, write it down, and repeat.*

# CHAPTER 4

## ~THE DEMISE OF RELATIONSHIPS~

There are several things that can destroy any relationship, but probably the most destructive is unforgiveness. Regardless of whether the alleged offense is true or not, wrong or right, the person who is not willing to forgive literally hinders that relationship and prevents it from being productive. Furthermore, how can anyone expect God to forgive a person if they are not willing to forgive others? Read Colossians 3:13 and Mark 11:25-26.

## Seeds of Destruction

Do you know that something as minor as a misunderstanding has destroyed many relationships? It has destroyed marriages, families, friends, and even relationships between brethren. Unfortunately, most people would rather live with the misunderstanding than try to resolve the issues by just communicating with one another. Some people would even deny there is anything wrong but will often tell other people how they truly feel, not knowing they are sowing a seed of destruction into their heart. God will hold YOU accountable for every seed of destruction you sow. Seeds of destruction can cause a person to be upset, despise, hate, or even kill another person.

Where does a seed of destruction come from? Good question. I'm glad you asked. Destruction originates from the nature of sin which dwells in man. This sin nature is a nature that's full of wickedness, and its only purpose is to destroy. The good news is Jesus Christ died on the cross for your sin and to deliver you from this terrible nature of sin.

Let's look at a few biblical relationships that went bad due to a "seed of destruction."

**Lucifer and God** Isaiah 14: 12-14 describes how Lucifer wanted to exalt himself above the stars of God and be like the most High God. This "seed of destruction" in the form of pride and jealousy got Lucifer kicked out of heaven. This same seed of destruction dwells in the earth today and continues to destroy relationships.

**Cain and Abel** We have all heard the story of Cain and Abel in the book of Genesis. It was Cain's jealousy which led to his anger, his anger led to his hatred, and his hatred led him to murder, killing his brother Abel. Fundamentally, it all started with Cain's broken relationship with God. Thinking he could just offer God anything and that God would accept it was totally wrong from the beginning. We cannot think we can serve God any kind of way, and He will be pleased with us; that is so far from the truth.

**Saul and David** In the book of 1st Samuel, we read how Saul, the King of Israel, became very jealous of David and tried to kill him several times; but there is so much more to understand about this situation. Think of it like this. When the enemy causes a disturbance between you and God's anointed person, he is trying to separate you from what's good for you. For example, in 1st Samuel 16:14-23, Saul had become oppressed by an evil spirit. A servant of Saul's tells him about David:

> *Then answered one of the servants, and said, Behold, I have seen a son of Jesse the Beth-lehemite, that is cunning in playing, and a mighty valiant man, and a man of war, and prudent in matters, and a comely person, and the Lord is with him.* I Samuel 16:18 (KJV).

So, Saul calls for David, and David comes to Saul and plays his harp for Saul. David is ministering God's goodness unto Saul in music, with God's anointing. The evil spirit departed from Saul, and Saul was refreshed. The scripture says that Saul loved David. It is obvious that Saul saw the good in David and how valuable it was to keep him nearby.

However, in the 18th chapter of 1st Samuel, verses 8 & 9, Saul becomes jealous of David which leads to hatred, and subsequently, an attempt on David's life (very similar to Cain and Abel). First Samuel, Chapter 19, verse 1 is where Saul puts a *hit* on David, the same anointed man of God who had ministered the goodness of the Lord unto him.

As I said before, the enemy's job is to separate you from what's good for you. Saul's and Cain's demise was a direct reflection of their relationship with God. The enemy will always take advantage of any Christian who will not commit their heart unto God. You have to stay in constant fellowship with the Father and avoid the sin nature that empowers seeds of destruction at all costs. Read Galatians 5:19-20 for more information about the sin nature and how it hinders your walk with God.

Testimony

*In May 2015, I was tested within my extended family that could have very well cost me my job. Without going into details, I want to highlight what was most important about this ordeal. Regardless of the challenges I experienced – it was the result that was absolutely rewarding. When the incident began, it immediately resulted with an investigation of me and my wife, which lasted approximately three weeks. I remember hearing the Holy Spirit say to me, "You need to keep your heart clear of this because you're going to lead her (this family member) back to the Father." In November 2015, we had a family meeting with an attempt to restore our relationship. Before the meeting began, I was instructed by the Holy Spirit to ask this family member to forgive me. My first thought was I didn't do anything wrong. But, I was reminded it's not about me. It's about restoring relationship back to the Father. Everything the Holy Spirit said would happen at this meeting, happened. Relationships were restored between the family and with the Father. Now, I get to enjoy family relationship as intended.*

The more we increase our fellowship with God, the more we'll began to see who He is in us, and the less we'll see of ourselves, and the less likely we'll fall prey to the seed of destruction.

Let us pray:

*Father, I thank You for giving your children wisdom on how to deal with seeds of destruction. I thank You for Your grace and strength to use this wisdom; without Your grace and strength it cannot be done, Amen.*

## How to Avoid Seeds of Destruction

The enemy's most opportune time to sow his seed of destruction is when a believer fails to strengthen his relationship with the Lord. The same deceitful lies the enemy used since the beginning of time are the same lies he uses now. There's another popular saying, *"The game hasn't changed, just the players"*. The enemy is always seeking whom he may sow his seed of destruction into. As mentioned earlier, he wants to separate you from what's good for you and to you.

There are many other examples of broken relationships throughout the Bible. In each broken relationship, there is that one person or group of people whom the seed of destruction was sown into. Once the seed of destruction is sown into your heart, it's just a matter of time before the separation comes. There's only one way to avoid the enemy's seed, and that's by staying in constant fellowship with the Lord. Jesus told Peter in Luke 22: 31-32,

> *And the Lord said, Simon, Simon, behold, Satan hath desired to have you, that he may sift you as wheat: But I have prayed for thee, that thy faith fail not: and when thou art converted, strengthen thy brethren* (KJV).

The word "sift" literally means to separate. The enemy was trying to separate Peter from the Lord, but Jesus said that he was praying for Peter.

Say this out loud: *The enemy's number one plan is to separate me from the goodness of the Lord.*

As you continue your walk with the Lord, always be mindful of this, so when you are offended; particularly, with someone of the household of faith; i.e., the Pastor, the elders, or the brethren, know that the enemy is trying to *sift* you from the goodness of the Lord.

Here's something else to think about—have you ever had an unpleasant thought about what someone has said to you? Sometimes, it seems to just stay on your mind day after day. Do you remember the feeling you had during that time when that thought occupied your mind? I like to refer to it as the "ill feeling" or the "ugly feeling". It is certain to come around whenever there is a continuous pattern of an unpleasant thought in your mind. The unpleasant thought itself can cause the "ill feeling" or the "ugly feeling" to come, but to allow the unpleasant thought to linger in your mind more than it should will cause the "ill feeling" to increase and possibly result in a separation. The best way to avoid these terrible feelings is to first, go to the Lord in prayer and give it completely to Him. Secondly, express how you felt about what was said to you to the other person. Hopefully, the other person is a mature enough believer to simply apologize, ask for forgiveness, and all will be well.

Another way the enemy will try to sow his seed of destruction is through other people's hurt. For example, let's say you are a believer who pays his tithes and offerings faithfully. You also work in the ministry, attend church throughout the week, and attend all the church conferences. Leaders and others in the church notice your faithfulness and commend you for it. Praise the Lord!

Now, let's say you have asked the church to assist your child with a scholarship to attend college. As a matter of fact, your family and friends have suggested to you that you ask your church for financial help. However, when you ask the church for financial help, you're told they don't have a scholarship program. When you try to explain to your family and friends that the church doesn't have any scholarships, they become irate and begin reminding you of all the things you do for the church. This is where the enemy tries to use the hurt of other people to sow his seed of destruction.

You must be extremely careful how to process their convincing words which are the result of their own hurt. Although your loved ones and friends mean well, and they're just expressing how they feel, you must remember to see the real purpose of what they are saying and the affect it can have on your walk with the Lord if the offense should enter your heart. This is where you truly must realize where YOUR help comes from,

> *I will lift up mine eyes unto the hills, from whence cometh my help. My help cometh from the LORD, which made heaven and earth.* Psalms 121:1-2 (KJV).

Also, Philippians 4:19 says,

> *But my God shall supply all your need according to His riches in glory by Christ Jesus* (KJV).

By realizing this truth, you will guard your heart against the seed of destruction. It is imperative that you know the Word and maintain your fellowship with God in all things. Don't allow negative thoughts to occupy your mind continually, or they will create those weird feelings we talked about earlier. Speak against those thoughts with the Word of God and immediately give yourself over to the presence of God, and you will overcome all the tricks of the enemy.

Let us pray:

*Father, we thank You for Your wisdom given unto man upon their requests unto You. Your word says that if we lack wisdom let us ask of You, but we should ask in faith. We thank You for the understanding of why we should constantly be in fellowship with Your Spirit and very mindful of Your word.*

*Lord, help us to separate ourselves unto You more and more, so that we can increase our relationship with You, Amen.*

## Reflection

*Is there someone you need to forgive but find it very challenging? If so, receive the Father's grace and strength. Forgiveness is not based on your individual ability but on your ability to allow the Holy Spirit to help you to forgive.*

## The Renewed Mind

We have all learned to live according to the world's way of doing things. Our thought process during an unpleasant, unfavorable circumstance or situation will often leave us troubled or emotionally stressed.

As a human race, we are connected to each other more than we realize. As we grow up into young adults and adults, we behave or conduct ourselves based on how we perceive or understand a matter. For the most part, we react or respond to certain situations from what we've seen or heard in our upbringing or in our present-day living. This is how we've become who we are and how we live our life according to this world's way of doing things.

For many years, we have lived our lives in this manner, becoming accustomed to tragedies that are the result of this "learned" way of living. One worldly principle that has devastating consequences that many of us are familiar with is *retaliation:*" You do me wrong; I'll do you wrong" This has been the mindset for centuries and still remains today. We've even given this principle other names, such as *getting even* or *getting revenge*. This is one example of the "learned" way of living. It is what we have seen and/or heard while growing up and has caused us to learn and adopt these principles into our own lives. Living a life that reflects these principles is living a life that is a lie, deceptive, and full of destruction.

Most of the things you have learned, whether they came from the media or advice from a friend or family member, might have been in direct contradiction to God's Word. If so, you are being led by this world's way of doing things which will cause you to fail—it is inevitable.

Divorce is a worldly phenomenon that is often spurred by a mindset which is governed by the world. People are getting divorced and remarried as if they are trading in their old cars for a new one. Most couples are getting divorced simply because they don't like or love each other anymore. The strangest thing is when a celebrity gets a divorce, it makes the news, as if divorce is being glorified. Here is a list of very petty arguments people make for getting a divorce: my spouse has gained weight, my spouse is getting too old, my spouse doesn't make enough money, or my spouse does not love me anymore.

These sentiments stem from a *false knowledge* and a *deceptive understanding* that has misled, misguided, confused, and blinded the minds of people for a very, very long time. It has given mankind an unrealistic view of marriage, or a mindset that is against the truth of how marriage was originally designed.

Just because we have lived a certain way for so long, that does not mean it is the way we are supposed to continue to live. It is simply the way we know how to live. However, when the "Truth" is revealed, you will be challenged to make the right decision. In the book of Daniel, Chapter 1, verse 5 it states, *"And the king appointed them a daily provision of the king's meat, and of the wine which he drank: so, nourishing them three years, that at the end thereof they might stand before the king"* (KJV).

Notice how long the king wanted Daniel and his friends to live under his daily provision to effectively use them in his Babylonian (world's) way of doing things— for three years. How long have you been living according to this world's way of doing things, contrary to God's Word? Can you see the negative effects it has had on your life? Transitioning from one mindset to another will be a challenge to any new believer. Remember, you've been living a certain way for so long. Still, with God's grace and mercy and with an intimate fellowship with the Father, you will be victorious. You will begin to live on purpose and live out the will of God for your life. It's so awesome to know and live out your purpose on this earth!

In that same Chapter 1 of Daniel, verses 12-20, Daniel persuaded the people to allow him and his friends to eat pulse (vegetables) and drink water for ten days to prove themselves against the countenance of the king's children. After the ten days were completed, Daniel and his friends' appearance was in a much better condition than the king's children. God's favor and His blessings were upon Daniel and his friends.

For the next ten days, whatever is troubling you or whatever negative thought you've been dealing with, I want you to find your matter in God's Word. Study scriptures dealing with that issue in different translations—the King James Version, the Amplified Version, the New International Version, etc. Speak these verses throughout the day to yourself. I also want you to pray and thank God every day for your deliverance, regardless of what you see presently. I assure you if you are diligent in your seeking, God will reward you for your diligence.

Romans 8:6 says that being "spiritually minded" is life and peace. When we transition in our thinking, we will eventually transition to the knowledge of who God is. We must spend time daily in God's word as well as time in His presence to truly know God for ourselves. Remember, in the book of Daniel when the king wanted Daniel and his friends to partake in his provision, _daily_, for three years? We must spend time in God's word and in His presence, _daily_, so that we will know His word and intimately know Him. When we do this, we will begin to speak as His children as He has created us to do because we were created in His image. This is how we renew our minds to God's will and His way of doing things.

## *Study to show yourself approved*

*Take a moment to reflect on a recent hardship in your life. What occupied your mind the most? Was it the problem? Or was it your relationship with the Father? Practice acknowledging and cultivating a relationship with the Father more. Doing so will help you experience more of His peace in you. To get further revelation, find someone in the Old and New Testament who demonstrated peace while going through a difficult time.*

# CHAPTER 5

## ~PERFECT LOVE DEFINED~

Perfect love wants to celebrate your return home, back to the heavenly Father. Consider the story of the prodigal son. When he decided to return home, he thought he would come back to an unwelcome environment where he would have to make amends for his sins upon his return home. But, to his surprise, his return turned out to be a celebration. The response of his father was transformative, and love was at the center of it.

Read below how the dialogue and interaction happened.

> *When he was still a long way off, his father saw him. His heart pounding, he ran out, embraced him, and kissed him. The son started his speech: 'Father, I've sinned against God, I've sinned before you; I don't deserve to be called your son ever again.' But the father wasn't listening. He was calling to the servants, 'Quick. Bring a clean set of clothes and dress him'...* Luke 15:21-24 The Message (MSG)

**Pay Attention to How the Father's Love Works**

When the son started his prepared speech to his father in The Message translation, it states, *"But the Father wasn't listening."* Instead, the father was more concerned about making changes and preparing for a celebration. That is what the love of God does—**it**

**brings the correct changes in your life and prepares you for a celebration!**

What may appear as if the father were ignoring his son, was the father's way of not entertaining the content of the son's conversation, which only reminded the son of the wrong he had done. A loving father does not want his children to be constantly reminded of the wrong they have done. So, the father's next action was instructing his servant to bring new clothing to dress his son.

There were three important changes that transpired during the son's return that we, as believers, especially those that return to the Father should take heed to:

1. **Change what comes out of your mouth.** The father did not want his son to be mindful of his sin. Rather than dwelling on your mistakes and discussing them with others, align your words with the Words that God says about you.

2. **Change your way of thinking.** Do not allow your troubled past to have an impact on your present day or hinder your future by allowing negative thoughts to dwell in your mind.

3. **Change your garment.** Receive the garments that have been made available to you (Isaiah 61:3). Get rid of the old and put on the new.

## Intimacy With the Father

These changes are necessary as you prepare for celebration. How can anyone celebrate if they're troubled by thoughts of their past? The father wanted to celebrate his son's return; therefore, it was necessary for the son to experience unconditional love to comfort him beyond his troubled past.

## Like Father, Like Son

What if we showed the same love to those who have wronged us as the father did to his prodigal son? If, when the person starts to apologize for his or her wrong doing, you interrupt them to reach out to them to hug them and celebrate the fact that they are there. Then you say to them, "Let's just praise God and give Him the glory!" What would be the impact on that person to experience this kind of love? This kind of love leads to true intimacy.

The beauty of intimacy with Father, God is it creates all things necessary for your entire being. There's nothing else in this world that can fulfill your inner-being like an intimate relationship with the Father. As a believer, it helps you go far beyond a mere mental relationship into a more meaningful, purposeful, personal relationship. There is a difference between human understanding, which is reliant upon worldly information, and spiritual understanding, which calls for intimacy and relationship with God. Intimacy means that you "know" a person beyond their physical attributes.

The word "know" or "knew" means to produce. Your intimate relationship with the Father should always cause you to produce His will on this earth.

The rewards of an intimate relationship provide the upmost assurance, comfort, and peace. There are certain things that transpire through an intimate relationship with the Father which I believe will not happen any other way.

*Here's an opportunity to renew yourself right now. Say this with me: "Father, today I renew myself to You. I thank You for Your mercy and Your love. I thank You that You always celebrate me. Help me make this my new reality. From this day forward, I will only speak Your Words over my life – Amen."*

## The Ministry of Reconciliation

*All of this is a gift from our Creator God, who has pursued us and brought us into a restored and healthy relationship with Him through the Anointed. And He has given us the same mission, the ministry of reconciliation, to bring others back to Him"* 2 Corinthians 5:18 The Voice Bible

The ministry of reconciliation is where every Christian must allow the Holy Spirit to mature him or her to become the vessel where Christ's love can flow through unhinderedly. As a believer operating in this ministry, you must do two things immediately and effectively:

1. Know how to acknowledge the Lord quickly (Proverbs 3:6), and

2. Know how to cast your cares quickly (I Peter 5:7)

The ministry of reconciliation requires God's grace, strength, love, and forgiveness to operate effectively. You are like a doorway to heaven for unbelievers; and God's love, mercy, and forgiveness flows through you without anything hindering it. There is absolutely no room for "self." "Self" will only get in the way of this ministry.

By God's grace and strength and the indwelling of the Holy Spirit - you'll be able to function *heavenly* in this ministry, and you don't need a title, just a willing vessel to be used for His glory.

Testimony:

*A lesson on love. In 2011, I began receiving a teaching on unconditional love by the Holy Spirit. He shared with me how to love unconditionally and how it would impact people. He reminded me it is the goodness of the Lord that causes man to repent (Romans 2:4), and if I did what he told me, I would get the same results. This lesson with the Holy Spirit seemed like it lasted two weeks. As with other lessons, now came the test, of course, to show how much I had been paying attention.*

*Love tested. One day while attending church service, an unpleasant situation happened that involved someone yelling at my mother, my wife, and myself. Initially, I wanted to slam that person on his neck, but I thank God for His divine intervention – His peace rules. My wife was upset and was ready to leave church. But, we stayed and enjoyed the service.*

*The next day, the Holy Spirit instructed me to bless that individual who yelled at my family. I shared with my wife what the Holy Spirit had instructed me to do. When she said she agreed with the Holy Spirit's idea – to me that was a confirmation.*

***Love overcomes.*** *That following Wednesday while in service, I saw that person in the same aisle where the unpleasant situation happened. I walked up to him and said I want to bless you. I handed him an envelope with a gift for him and his wife to go to a nice restaurant. When he received the envelope, opened it up and saw what was in the envelope – tears began falling down his face, and he said, "Man, look what you're doing to me." I was floored at what was happening in front of me. This was the result of showing love to someone, even though he might have done wrong to me. At this precise moment, I heard the Holy Spirit say again to me," If you do what I tell you, you'll get the same results."*

I now live my life from this perspective—this spiritual truth. As Christians, we know this is how the Father loves us. Regardless of how we may fall short at times – **He is always good to us and ready to forgive** (Psalms 86:5). We, His children, must imitate our Father to all people. We must be good to all, forgive all, and show mercy to all. That is imitating our beloved Father, Jehovah God.

The unpleasant experience between that individual and myself had to happen for several reasons; however, I will only elaborate on one. Remember when I said the Holy Spirit was teaching me how to love others **unconditionally**? If I never use what's on the inside of me, how will I ever know whether it's effective? When knowledge meets application (experience), that's when the faith, *in you*, takes a step. You've now witnessed the power that's working within you. When you've taken enough steps in faith, it builds such a momentum that the enemy can do nothing to stop you.

*The steps of a good man are ordered by the Lord: and he delighteth in his way Psalm 37:23 (KJV).*

I am happy to report this brother and I have become good friends, as true brothers in Christ. He has invited me and my family to his lovely home multiple times.

### Walking in the Resurrection Power of Jesus

Would you agree that Lazarus walked with Jesus? The word of God even described them as being friends. However, Lazarus' greatest impact for the Kingdom was **not** when he just walked with Jesus, but when he walked in the **resurrection** of Jesus Christ.

**Notice what transpired when the Pharisees (Chief priests) met Lazarus in John 12:9-11:**

*When the word got out that Jesus was not far from Jerusalem, a large crowd came out to see him, and they also wanted to see Lazarus, the man Jesus had raised from the dead. This prompted the chief priests to seal their plans to do away with both Jesus and Lazarus, for his miracle testimony was incontrovertible (not able to be denied or disputed) and was persuading many of* the Jews living in Jerusalem to believe in Jesus." The Passion Translation

*Much people of the Jews therefore knew that he was there: and they came not for Jesus' sake only, but that they might see Lazarus also, whom he had raised from the dead. But the chief priests consulted that they might put Lazarus also to death; because that by reason of him many of the Jews went away and believed on Jesus.* John 12:9-11 (KJV)

Notice in verse 10 how the chief priests wanted to kill Lazarus and in verse 11 notice why they wanted to kill Lazarus - **because he caused many to believe**. I believe it was the resurrection power of Jesus Christ which Lazarus was walking in that had a major impact on the people who were witnesses of this glorious power. As believers, we too can walk in this same resurrection power of Jesus Christ, but He must first be accepted as Lord and Savior; afterwards, we must learn to come to an end of "Self."

## Coming to the End of "Self."

One of the most difficult things to do as a Christian is to come to the end of yourself. It's called, "dying to yourself." We've become so used to doing things our way that we often get in the way of what God wants to do through us. It is only when a believer walks in the resurrection of the Lord Jesus Christ can he experience a transformation like never before.

The Bible tells us that we are in heavenly places in Christ Jesus in Ephesians 2:6,

> *And hath raised us up together and made us sit together in heavenly places in Christ Jesus..." (KJV).*

This is what I call a *transition* before the "Transition." We, as believers, don't have to wait to transition to our heavenly home to experience what the *transition life* offers. The moment you accept Jesus Christ as your personal Savior, you've transitioned. Now comes the cultivation of this relationship through intimacy which will allow you to come to the end of yourself, which then positions you to walk in His resurrection power.

## Living From Heaven to Earth

As believers, it is extremely important that we go far beyond conversion or just accepting salvation. We cannot stop at conversion, or we will miss out on the main purpose of relationship with the Trinity (the Father, the Son, and the Holy Spirit.)

This is where the enemy has fooled many believers—by failing to cultivate this very important relationship. This is where increasing your understanding of relationships happens. Your sensitivity to the Holy Spirit increases as you spend time cultivating a relationship with Him. It's at this point that you begin to live heaven on earth.

## Having Eyes to See

> *The servant of the man of God woke up early and went outside. There he saw a great army, along with many horses and chariots, encircling Dothan. Elisha's servant: Ah! Master, what are we going to do now? Elisha: Have no fear. We have more on our side than they do. (praying) O Eternal One, I ask You to allow my servant to see heavenly realities. The Eternal awakened Elisha's servant so that he could see. This is what he saw: the mountain was covered with horses and chariots of fire surrounding Elisha."* 2 Kings 6:15-17 (The Voice Bible)

Notice the concern from Elisha's servant when he saw what he thought to be trouble. But, more importantly, notice the other (heaven's) reality Elisha helped him to see. There are always two realities: From Heaven to earth or from earth to Heaven. I pray you see things from Heaven's reality. This is where total victory awaits you.

This can only be accomplished by the help of the Holy Spirit; any other way will cause you to come up short and bring forth much unnecessary frustration.

Through this intimate relationship with the Lord, it allows you to see difficult situations from heaven's perspective; it allows you to hear _more of_ what the Holy Spirit is saying to you in difficult situations. It allows you to speak (decree and declare) what the Word says when confronted with difficult situations; it protects you from anxiety, depression, confusion, and hopelessness. It will position you to live in God's reality for your life. All that the Word of God says you can do – **you can do.**

**Absolute Truths.**

The following absolute truths will cause you to prosper in your relationships with other brothers and sisters in the household of faith. Apply them liberally and allow the Holy Spirit to guide your interactions as you die to yourself and love with an unconditional love.

**Brothers:** associate yourselves with other men who love the Lord. If you do this, you will benefit from positive male role models that will demonstrate how to be godly fathers and husbands.

**Sisters:** associate yourselves with other women who love the Lord not with women who spend more time gossiping than praying. Women who love the Lord will provide an excellent example for you and teach you how to be a good wife and mother.

God created relationships and has given us the answers to have successful, meaningful, and purposeful relationships. No one has to fail at cultivating them. We will not be successful in relationships without the Father in the center of them. There are no perfect relationships, but God can perfect in you the ability to successfully relate to others in every area of your life (Ephesians 4:12).

In conclusion – to have right relationships with others, you must first have a right relationship with the Father. Allow the Holy Spirit to teach you how to cultivate a meaningful, purposeful relationship with the Father, and you will experience the most exciting, liberating, and gratifying life journey known to man. His attributes will flow through you, unhindered, causing others to encounter the greatest love in the history of humanity – **Jesus Christ!**

Let us pray: – *Father, I thank You for the ministry of reconciliation. I intentionally and purposely set myself in agreement to be a door-way that leads others to You. I receive Your grace, strength, and unconditional love to forgive others for wrong doing. I thank You for increasing my faith to live this life that You pre-ordained for me before the foundation of the world.*

**Amen.**

**SHALOM**

# ACKNOWLEDGEMENTS

I first want to thank the Lord for revealing to me that my purpose on earth is to write books that will bring honor and glory to Him. I thank Him for giving me dreams and inspiring me to write this book. When the Lord gave me the title for this book, I asked the Lord at least three to four times, please don't allow anyone to publish this book before I do. I truly thank Him for hearing and answering my prayer, as He always does. Amen.

There is a true saying that many people might not really understand or agree with. In this world nothing just happens; in other words, there are no coincidences. I live my life unto God with intention and on purpose; I am living out His will for my life. What I realized is God has strategically placed people in my life for one reason or another. The truth of the matter is certain things must happen, and certain people must help.

As my walk with Christ has evolved and caused me to be a better vessel unto God, this has improved my relationship with my dearly beloved and has prepared me for those whom God Jehovah had predestined for me to meet.

**My wife**:

Bertha, you epitomize what it means to be a "help meet". I thank you for your help in fulfilling God's will and purpose for my life. I've come to realize that you were graced to be my wife. I am so glad we met in 1989, and five months later we got married. I thought I knew what I was doing, but it was the Lord who put us together. The confirmation of this continues to reveal this truth from time to time. Your love for me reflects the love of the Lord in my life, and I am so thankful and grateful to have you. Thank you for allowing God to use you to minister to me as my very own, God-given, "help meet". I'll try to out-love you, you'll try to out-love me, and we'll have fun doing it. May we continue to spoil each other in God's awesome love. Amen.

**Mom & Pop:**

I want to thank my mom and pop, Emma and Frank Cannon, for their love and support on this project.

Mom, I thank you for introducing me to the Lord and to church at a very young age; it had a huge, ever-lasting impact on my life. I still remember how you would be praying so loudly in our home, making declarations unto the Lord. I can remember when I was having trouble with life, and I came to you with my concern, and you said, "Ricky, you just need to give yourself to the Lord." I thank you for leading me to our Lord and Savior, Jesus Christ. Amen. I love you, mom.

Pop, I thank you for teaching me and demonstrating to me how to be a real man and how to provide for my family. I remember how you would tell me about my friends who didn't have any money yet would always come around me if I had money to give them. It was only when I didn't have any money that they didn't come around. I thank you for giving me guidance through life. I love you, sir.

## My family:

I wish to express my love and gratitude to all my children: Katina, Ericka, Marchone, Ontonio (lil' Rick), and Kaneisha. God has an awesome call on our lives, and His "will" will be done on earth as it is in heaven, Amen.

To my grand babies: Tajae, Aariyah, Zayani, Gabrielle, Delonte, Xaidyn, and Issa – you are my continual joy of the Lord.

To my Godson: Walter Forbes –You have been an example of how to love, support, and encourage the other siblings; I thank you for all you have done.

To my Goddaughter: April Morris – Stay sweet princess. Sugar doesn't have anything on you.

## My current Pastors:

Pastors Tony and Cynthia Brazelton – Glory to God – Hallelujah to the Most High God! I thank you for laying down your lives for Christ and how you are committed to His will being done on earth as it is in heaven. I thank you for sharing your heavenly encounters with God's presence; it has captured my utmost attention and has allowed me to pursue after God like never before. I thank God for the gift you are to the body of Christ. Amen.

**Victory Christian Ministry International (VCMI):**

I love and appreciate y'all so much. There are so many wonderful people to name who have been instrumental in my walk with the Lord. I couldn't possibly think of everyone, so without offending anyone, I'll just say – thank you, and may God bless you. Amen.

**Victory Bible College:**

To my tremendously anointed classmates "God's Image in the Earth." (GIITE)

Our tears were sown in the earth, giving each one of us a stronger foothold assuring the kingdom of God and His will is carried out. Since the great transformation that happened between 2010 – 2015, a permanent mark has forever been set in this earth that can never be erased or undone.

**Special thanks to Etelle Carson, Marvin Williams, Marvin Armstrong, Patrick Barnes, John Petty and Jeffrey Cottle for being my first audience - reading the material and providing awesome constructive feedback.**

My prayer to all is that you will have multiple encounters with the presence of God to the point where you will literally cry out unto Him to reveal to you more of His captivating, passionate-burning (can't help yourself) love. Amen.

Shalom.

You can reach me at:
a.matthews01@verizon.net

Special gratitude to ZION Publishing House for their outstanding work and commitment to excellence in making sure my reading material was grammatically correct, proper biblical verbiage was used and the book was easy to comprehend to all readers.

## ABOUT ZION PUBLISHING HOUSE

ZION Publishing House is a family-owned publishing company based in Southern California and Washington, DC. ZION helps Christian authors tell their stories by providing an affordable alternative to traditional publishing. Our mission is to maintain a platform that educates and empowers independent Christian authors. We do this by cultivating talent in the inspirational and self-help genres for novice and experienced authors. The path to publishing can be daunting and extremely complex. We take pride in taking our clients by the hand and walking them through the publishing process to ensure they not only have a high-quality product that resonates with the reader, but they understand the many facets of the publishing industry and what it means to be a published author.

If you are a writer looking for an affordable path to publishing, visit our website at www.zionpublishinghouse.com to learn more.